The Day the Skies Opened to Give Me the Water I Needed

by Maskarm Haile & Ishan Dub

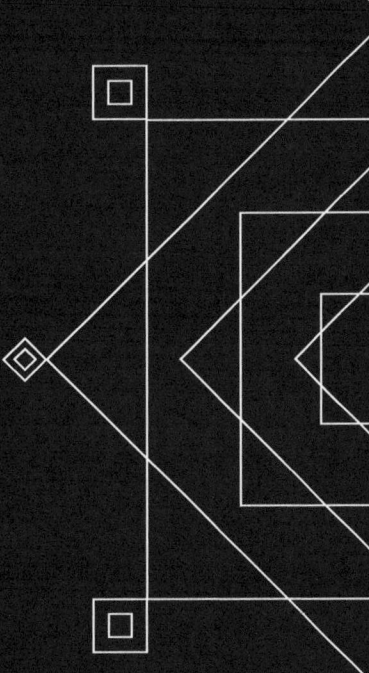

Maskarm:
Speaking to dub,
Speaking through h.i.m.

 AFREEKAN DUB BIOGRAPHIES#

Book cover and graphic design by
DUBZAINE

Textual engineering by
PRASONIK

Conceptual book layout by
WHEN VISION MEETS DUB ARCHITECTURE

This is an autonomous production created by • Atuadub • TFTT • IR

Contact Atuadub TFTT:
jahdub.ghost.stories@gmail.com

Maskarm Haile can be reached by:
maskarmh@gmail.com

PUBLISHED BY TFTT-IR • ATUA DUB
© 2021 • 978-1-927801-26-0
TORONTO • ADDIS ABABA • SÃO PAULO

★

VISION MEETS
DUB ARCHITECTURE

◉ IR

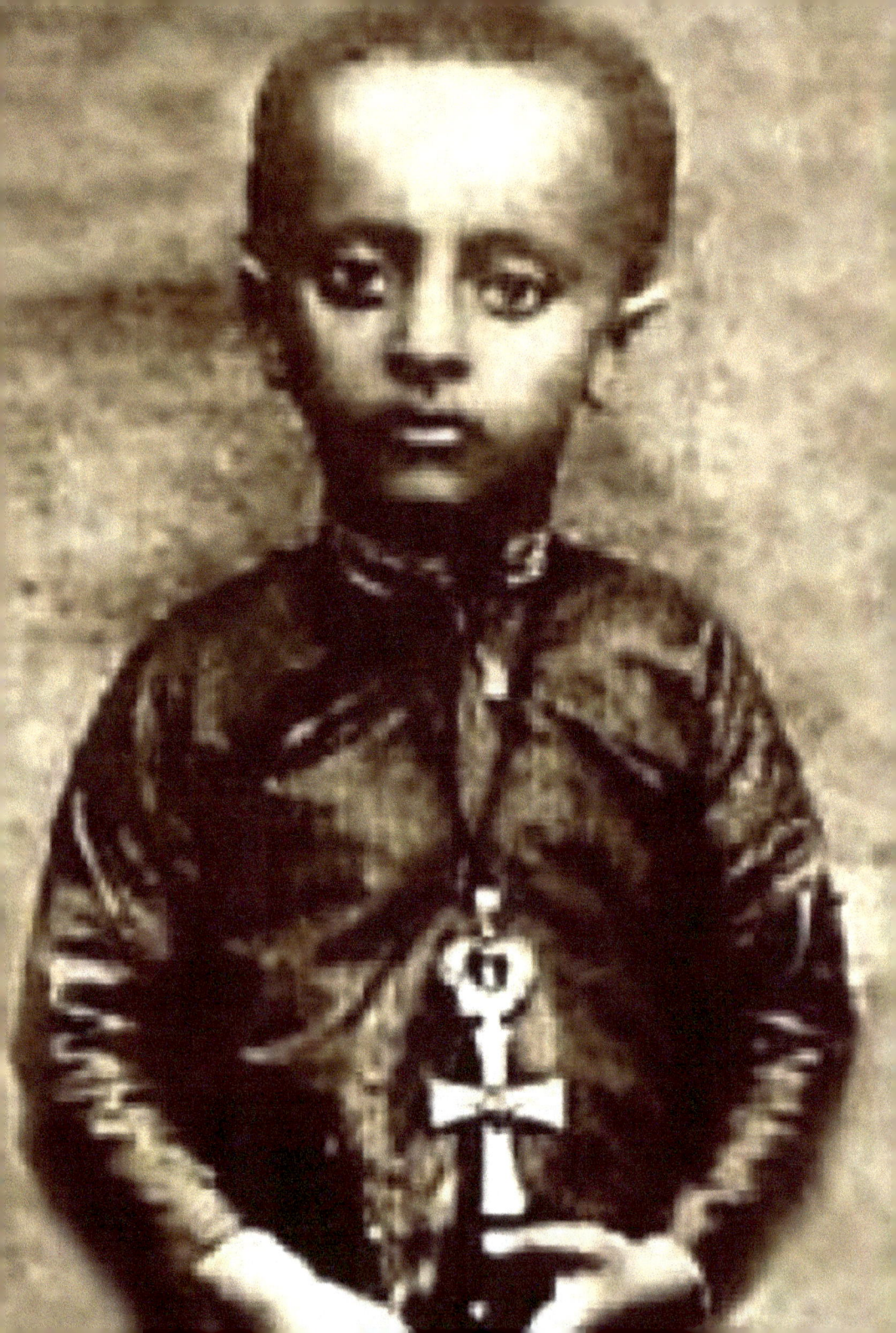

Preface

The subtitle for this book "Maskarm: Speaking to dub, Speaking through h.i.m." came from a **dream**.

We were astounded when we recalled the dream because we felt it came from a time and space completely outside of our own consciousness. We even saw the punctuation marks in "h.i.m." It was not the type of title we would have thought of on our own. We felt if it came that way, there must be a higher purpose, so we have kept it and used it for this book.

Lij Tafari Makonnen (circa age 3), Haile Selassie King of Ethiopia as a child

Image of Maskarm on the cover taken
in the volcanic Afar region in Ethiopia.

1 — 9

In the Forest

2 — 17

After the Forest

3 — 25

The Day the Heavens Opened,
The Day the Skies Opened Up
To Give Me The Water I Needed.

4 — 35

The Veil - The Gift

In the Forest

Lalibela, Ethopia.
Photo by Maski.

Here
I was in
Karura forest
in Nairobi,
Kenya.

When I walk in this forest, the first thing that impacts me is that it is like I'm being immediately reunited with something I have had a deep yearning for, while simultaneously being revitalised by the fresh air. Like a gift, I am receiving the pure oxygen that is being offered up by the surrounding ancient trees.

I looked up at the tall trees and as is my custom when I enter a new place, I said

"Hello, my name is Maski and I am here to learn."

At that moment, I was hit by an overwhelming feeling of being recognized. It was as if the wind and the trees were conspiring to welcome me in a language I could hardly understand. I bowed my head in gratitude for that warm welcome.

Already, I felt I was in the midst of various sacred conversations.

By my side were two women: amazing healers, who were ready with their counsel for me. At the same time, I felt I was also having a conversation with living, ancient beings who presented themselves in the form of these trees.

We were speaking deeply on the subject of healing. I was so conscious of breathing in the fresh air and so focused on the act of breathing that I said to my companions Yami and Anika:

"I literally feel like I'm breathing for the first time in a long time."

I stopped, momentarily placed my hand on my heart. I realised that in many ways, I didn't know where I was in my life. I was chronically fatigued, I was confused, and at the bottom of this, I was truly wondering if this was to be the end of my life on this earth. I could not see what I could do to move things forward.

Suddenly Yami exclaimed, "Look at that over there!"

I glanced quickly and caught a glimpse of what seemed to be a deer. I felt an excitement inside. I was determined to follow the direction it went even though it might be going off the main trail. As I did so, I felt a sense of immediate happiness!

With this renewed energy came another realisation: why couldn't and why didn't I simply ask for something - anything!

I now realised that at that moment, my brain was so fogged. I could not even concentrate on defining what I needed. There was just too much pain.

There have been moments where I could see remnants of my soul as fragments of rocks lying in a pile at the bottom of a cliff, literally made from smashing myself against immovable walls, whether those walls were formed by culture, tradition, beliefs or simply habit.

Yet, I did manage to realize that I was here in this place that abounded with ancestral spirits and in many ways, what better place to ask for their guidance?

I realized I was not even asking for healing from this life. I was grateful for the life I had been given. I loved life. I trusted life. I followed my own magic. I lived this way despite people being completely perplexed and at times utterly disbelieving my attitude to life. So, at this moment, my only wish was to prepare and finalize things so I could leave this earth cleanly. I wanted to clean up my karma.

As I sat in this forest, I watched the sunlight pierce through the tall, ancient trees. The sunlight invoked various memories, and one of them was directly related to thoughts on the relationship of karma to my life.

Whenever I meditate on sunlight, my university time in India always comes up. Sunlight in India has its own very distinct visual frequency and warmth and somehow I also always connect it to the famous astrologer who visited my auntie's house in India. This man, who predicted the assassination of Indira Gandhi, the Indian prime minister, had been invited to my auntie's house to give her a reading.

My host who I lovingly referred to as "auntie" even though she was not a blood relative, is a remarkable and wealthy Brahmin Indian woman with an enormous heart. Not only had she opened her house to give me a place to live while I was studying, but she also provided opportunities for numerous women of different social classes, including some who in that current social climate were scorned by society.

I distinctly remember when she said to the famed astrologer, "Here is my daughter. Please give me a reading on her future."

Took my hand, examined it and also began working on his charts.

He told me things that at that moment I had absolutely no comprehension of.

Not only did he say that I had wisdom and an ability to heal others (which at that moment made absolutely no sense to me), but he also said that in life, I would have to overcome loneliness and habits of overthinking things.

So it becomes difficult to breathe again. Memories of being judged harshly, which I am ashamed to say led me to also being judgemental of others. Memories of feeling completely invisible and non-existent because I did not fit into the paradigm of what was "right" or "wrong," and because of that, I did not possess the material "things" or job credentials considered important.

I sat in the forest desperately wanting to breathe completely and fully as I had been moments before these memories flooded over me.

After the Forest

Labyrinth in South Africa, a prayer and meditation walkway. Photo by Maski.

I wrote a book about the importance of having a dream and following our hearts.

I shared this freely so others could find things within themselves. I knew my story and path was not for everybody, but I deeply believed in the possibility that my story could inspire someone to follow their own path.

At book readings, it touched my heart when people came up to me and said "your story spoke to me." But what I wasn't talking to them about was the price we pay when we choose our own path. There was no time to talk about that.

Now I realized I needed to investigate the root causes of all the physical and spiritual difficulties I was currently undergoing and for that I knew I had to revisit my childhood in Ethiopia.

There was a elder woman who was a very significant figure in my childhood. Her name was Dubalech. She was of very dark complexion and with white hair, which I found stunningly beautiful. I secretly wished and waited for the day I would get grey hair like hers. She was the person who I visited almost daily because I felt that she knew how to comfort me.

One of the main reasons for this was we had something in common. We never spoke directly about it, but it was our hidden bond. This secret was the fact that we were both in contact with the spirit world. Now that I understand more, I realise that it was the ancestors who came and spoke to me. They came and spoke with me as a young child and I could call them whenever I needed their help or presence.

In my childhood, I immediately perceived that Dubalech had this same relationship with her ancestors. One of the subtle indicators for me was that before the start of our traditional coffee ceremony, I would notice her putting offerings like popcorn, bread, and injera on the ground for the ancestors. Being very mischievous, I would sometimes go and eat these offerings off the ground, and she would just smile gently and put down some more.

As a child, I quickly learnt the parameters of what I could and could not say about my communication with the ancestors. If I said I saw this and that in a dream, that was fine. If I said I saw this person in a waking vision or this was told to me by a spirit, it was made very clear to me that this was simply unacceptable.

This was the start of a process where an essential part of me was being suppressed with disapproval and the implied threat of punishment if I continued to publicly pursue and communicate about this. Now I realize that this suppression was one of the root causes of the debilitating illnesses I experienced later on.

However, with Dubalech, I knew I could be free to be my complete self, and so I craved her company.

She was married to someone who I remember as being a very jolly man. He would sometimes return home drunk and act up a bit. However, at that young age, I had no concept of what being drunk involved. Then one day, I went to their house searching for Dubalech, and when I opened the door, I saw the figure of her husband hanging. He had committed suicide.

I was really shocked. However, what also shocked me was that this man's spirit was speaking to me, even though I could see he was physically dead. He apologized to me for seeing him like that and tried to calm me down. He told me to return to my house, and I immediately did. I ran back to my house and was silent. No one had any notion of what I witnessed. Later on, when his body was discovered, everyone made a concerted effort to keep the news hidden from me, but I had already seen what I had seen.

Now I realize I had encountered one of several taboo subjects, which was suicide. It was not something to be discussed. It made people uncomfortable. Later on in my life, when I lost two friends to suicide, I again was witness to the fact that their family and friends really did not want to talk about it.

In my childhood, I also experienced sexual abuse at the hands of someone entrusted to take me to and from school. Once again, I knew even as a young child that this was a taboo subject. I never even tried to speak on it.

When things like this happened to me, things that I wanted to discuss, my usual approach was to first test the waters by saying a little bit and watching people's reactions. I would then make a decision whether or not to say more. In this case, I knew that I had to be completely silent. It took many years before I could begin to speak on it.

As an adult and someone who has worked as an intuitive healer and life coach, I have seen and felt the damage that is done when we remain silent about the traumatic things that occur to us. I know the damage it has caused me. Our physical illnesses often manifest from the unresolved spiritual and emotional issues we carry.

Childhood experiences caused me to suppress the childhood connection I had with my ancestors. I loved that connection when I was a child because with the communication I had with them, I never felt alone. This was incredibly important to me.

Now after my illness, I have made the conscious decision to embrace that ancestral connection and my life has become richer as a result.

The Day the Heavens Opened, The Day the Skies Opened Up to Give Me the Water I Needed.

Lake in a Indigenous reservation, Turtle Island. Photo by Maski.

I need to take a quiet pause in reflection, to back track and to flow downstream in my journey as I'm recounting it, so that you more completely understand The Day the Heavens Opened, the Day the Skies Opened to Give Me the Water I Needed.

Let me share with you a quiet conversation I had with One who was listening intently, someone seeking to give healing gifts to the world, and in their journey chose to listen to me.

So, I spoke to them, not to elicit pity, sympathy, remorse, or any related emotion. My story was my story and that was it. I did harbour the hope and desire that moments and lessons of my existence could be of help to others. So, I spoke quietly and without embellishment about the painful period I went through.

I now know that part of the physical pain I endured was due to fibromyalgia, a medical condition involving widespread chronic pain, extreme fatigue, and memory loss. The severity of the symptoms are linked to post-traumatic stress disorder.

Yet, as I battled with the pain, a non-human intervention came to my assistance.

Plant medicine arrived. It communicated with me and showed me the proper respectful protocols so I could reap the benefits of its healing powers. This last part was of quintessential importance.

It was shown to me that, for myself, the plants were strictly for medicinal purposes. This was especially the case when I was guided on how to use plant medicine to easy my pain.

My ancestral guides were very strict and explicit to me in regards to this plant. This was not something for me to use just for fun and enjoyment; it was just really for me to use for healing myself. So, part of my ritual of using the plant involved respectfully acknowledging its healing powers, requesting it to bestow some of that healing on me, and being grateful afterwards for the healing that was shared with me. This quiet, yet powerful, two-way channel of communication was essential for the way that plant medicine became such a fundamental tool for my healing and the easing of chronic pain.

When I honed into the channel of respectful communication with the plants, which was aided by my ancestral guides, they communicated with me what I needed and how the instructions would be transmitted about how to use the plants.

Suddenly, without any background knowledge and experience, I found myself making intricate, yet potent, tinctures from plants. Normally, I would think that the only way to procure these tinctures would be by directly going to purchase them at a homeopathic pharmacy. Yet, here I was making them at home and these tinctures were incredibly effective in easing my physical pain!

I never forget one of the dramatic moments, and what I now realise was one of the turning points of my recovery. It was the day I suddenly started a flurry of gardening. There I was suddenly so comfortable with my hands in the soil! I was planting all these medicinal herbs that I needed . I'm sure anyone who knew me previously might have been a bit shocked to see my new found adeptness with cultivation. Tilling the soil and after the proper respectful communication, utilising the plant medicine that came forth from the cultivation. It became a source and foundation of rejuvenation for me.

In the process and with conscious reflection, I realized how social taboos, emphasised by modern-day, profit-driven, big business pharmaceutical companies, have pushed us into the direction of popping pills when healing herbs were readily and cheaply available.

My heart filled with sadness knowing that those who were close to me were in great pain and how if I could be by their side, I could use my medicinal plant knowledge to ease their suffering.

There was also a direct correlation with my healing, my communication with plant medicine, and my visions of my ancestral guides.

From the hazy visions to crystal-clear visions and direct communication, I have a memory of a particularly painful moment. The intensity of the physical pain had literally thrown me to the ground. Everything was a blur through the absolute throbbing pain. I was alone by myself in my apartment, but through the pain I could see hazy visions of different ancestors: aunties, grandparents, and uncles sitting in a circle around me. It was like they were watching over me and simultaneously willing me to keep going, to hang on through the pain, to not give up!

I now realise another important signpost in my recovery. It was a day which was dramatic in many ways. A culmination of the two-track simultaneous process that was occurring through communication with plant medicine and with my ancestral guides.

One afternoon I had taken some plant medicine. I was in the company of an acquaintance who suggested we go to a beautiful park that had a river running through it. We arrived and I was sitting on the green grass close to the river bank.

Suddenly, everything changed. It was like I was transported to another location. I could have been in the midst of an enormous barren desert. There was blinding sunlight, but the sensation that registered most for me was that I felt so much heat! I felt so hot. My skin was burning, and I immediately felt a physical urge to take off all of my clothes and jump into the roaring river.

I managed to center myself and came to the rapid conclusion that in this public space and in the company of someone I did not know so well, this would not be the wisest thing to do. So instead, I kept myself calm and just put my bare feet into the cold river water. That helped a bit, but I was still so very conscious of the searing heat, a blinding white light, a feeling of something immense, but intangible, swirling and moving me around.

Something was happening. Something was about to happen. I knew this. I could feel this.

I also knew my ancestral guides were involved. Their presence was unmistakable. More and more of them were showing up. I felt almost like I was sheltering inside a house during the middle of a megaforce hurricane, hearing and feeling the force of gale-force rain wind battering the house and me sitting there, just waiting for the forces of nature to completely blow the roof right off.

Suddenly, my acquaintance said it was time for us to go. My calm exterior gave them no clue of all that I was experiencing at that moment.

Inside the car, I once again felt that searing heat all over my skin. It was unbelievably hot, and I desperately wanted relief. To ease the pain, I tried to regulate my breathing using my yoga practice. I felt like molten lava was flowing on my skin! My spirit was crying out, crying out for relief.

We reached the driveway of where I was staying. Suddenly, the sky turned grey and then black, and the most tumultuous intense flood of rain came pouring down from the sky. I got out of the car and stepped onto the driveway. I did not even attempt to enter the house.

I just sat down right there in the driveway and let the cooling water cascade onto my skin. The relief was incredible, yet intangible, because it was more than the disappearance of the searing heat. I looked up at the skies and I could feel the presence of so many ancestors. They had spoken. They had opened a gateway for me to communicate more directly with them.

From that day, they were constantly in my presence and the communication between us was crystal clear.

When I look back at this day, I remember it as the Day the Heavens Opened Up. The Day the Skies Opened Up and Gave Me the Water I Needed.

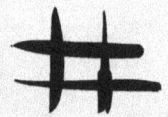

The Veil
-
The Gift

Fanjove Island,
Tanzania.
Photo by Maski.

Into the
magical
forest
I went.
A place on
sacred
Indigenous
land.

Soft pine cones and leaves crunched gently under my bare feet as I moved with wonderment through this place. I could feel the eyes of trees and plants upon my every step.

As I entered Wapani reserve, which is just outside Montreal, the Indigenous caretakers explained so carefully to me the importance of taking great care as I moved through the forest so as to not despoil it.

As I walked, my hands would occasionally brush the moist barks of trees, and I could smell a sublime sweetness in the air. Shapes and outlines of trees and saplings of different sizes seemed to imprint themselves in my mind's eyes. I was very conscious of the fact that I had stepped into another dimension and was now travelling through time.

There was one tree in particular that seemed to be calling out to me. It was very ancient! Part of it - a giant branch - crashed to the ground, but it had not detached itself from the tree trunk, even though logic might lead one to automatically arrive at that conclusion. Instead, its long elongated shape twisted and curled, forming beautiful and abstract images of curved wood that seemed sculptured by wind and water. Yet, it was still a living tree branch attached to the main tree branch.

I was pulled immediately to it. A force I can't describe propelled me to sit on the windblown leaves right beside this fallen, but living, branch. At this moment, I didn't feel like I had control of my actions, but I didn't fight it. I just surrendered and went with the flow. I removed my small backpack, sat on the ground in a cross legged lotus meditation pose, and closed my eyes.

I am uncertain of how to exactly describe when and what happened next.

All I know is that I had a communication
a conversation
a dialogue
with this Black man.

I can't describe his physical form clearly, but the one thing that was absolutely clear to my spirit was that his feet had trod on the soil of northern Ethiopia. I could literally see the remains of the earth from monasteries high, high up in the mountains still clinging to his bare feet.

The other thing I could see
oh so clearly
were his eyes
his eyelids
his eye lashes.

I mention this because several times during our communication tears would form in his eyes.

I would watch them form
and slowly descend
down his eyelids
and sometimes
hang in his eye lashes.

I remember someone speaking to me and saying they had heard an Iroquois elder say that tears were water washing the soul clean.

When I felt this man
I felt that he, like me,
wanted to wash his soul clean.
In low tones
I began to speak.

I felt both of us had
a curiosity and deeper desire
to know more about the unseen world.

In my heart, I felt that was one of our common purposes. I decided to start our spoken dialogue around this subject.

"When we arrived to this earth
we are in what I describe as sleeping mode.
We are going through the motions of life
and then we put a veil between us and the spirit world.

Numerous traditions talk about this veil.
However, because we can't touch it
and see the spirit world,
it makes it harder for people
to believe there is something more
because we want to be able to touch and see things.

Some religions try to placate
peoples' intuition of this
by saying

this is what we feel
when we die"

I could see him silently mouthing and repeating the term

"The veil, the veil…"

He stopped.

I saw him reach for a small pouch.
He opened it and I saw he was taking out tobacco.
He placed some on the ground in front of us.
I realized he was making an offering
and showing respect to the
the Indigenous spirits and guardians
and caretakers of the land we were on.

He bowed his head in silence and then he spoke directly to me, asking: "Well what can we do to dissolve the veil, so we can really see?"

I swept my arms in an arc
and pointed to all the nature
that surrounded us at that moment.

I said, "Well, one of the things I feel we can start with is where we are right now. We need to connect and pass more time with nature, with the Earth. We need to ground ourselves and spend more time with the Earth, and distance ourselves from the many distractions in our lives like the technological toys. These are deliberate distractions that sap our power.

A natural extension of us becoming more connected to Earth is that we can use Plant Medicines. By communicating with the Plant Medicines and then utilizing them in a respectful manner, we can dissolve the veil.

In a parallel manner, there are traditional ceremonies that serve this specific purpose. Music and sound can elevate our vibrations and this can also dissolve the veil.

I also know this happens when we are in the presence of those elevated spiritual beings like monks, medicine people, and imams. They can also raise our vibrations to a level where that veil which is blocking us from the spirit world is removed.
When we allow ourselves to be quiet
the veil opens up
because we are communicating with the inner self,
allowing spirits to come,

and we will receive signs
that will reveal themselves
through nature
through animals
through numerals
we start to see appearing.

We just need to be alert and with faith.
**And when spirits comes,
and they will come,
spirits don't tell you what to do.**

They give you choices
They emphasize our ability to discern
To discern what feels true to us!

We enhance our ability to discern through our connection with our own inner quiet.

This quiet can also dissolve the veil. Part of this very necessary introspection is asking

Who am I?
This is a fundamental question.

What do I really know about myself
I'm not the beginning
I'm not the end

It just needs us to say
"I know there is more
I'm uncertain where it will take me,
but i'm willing to explore it

There was a sweet Silence as he took in and absorbed my words. Then he spoke:

"I'm thinking about what you said about the veil.

It made me remember an account told by the Senegalese Saint and Scholar, Cheik Amadou Bamba. When he would have visions, he would see the Prophet Muhammed (peace be on him), but he would usually see him behind a veil of light.

But in that moment when he had the most important vision of his life, that veil of light was no longer there and he could see him directly. And at that moment he received transmissions that later on influenced generations and millions of people.

So when you speak on the importance of removing the veil, I really feel that within my spirit. I know my personal priority, which I feel encompasses removing the veil is to be as close to God as possible. All things flow through God.

A very learned spiritual teacher told me
that he often felt that the miracles connected to visions
occur when those who have received the vision
have had the complete trust and faith
to act on what they have seen.

I have to confess that
since I was child,
I have been receiving visions.

I also have to be very honest with myself and admit that I didn't have the faith and belief in myself to act on what I saw

as magnificent and stupendous
with Beauty
many of those visions were."

I could feel him shifting through past memories. I saw tears fall from his eyes.

After anchoring myself further in the silence, I said to him:

"We have given up so much of our power
sometimes it can be
first to our parents
then to community
then to relationships
then to institutions
then to larger society

There are many variations, but at the end of the day, we have lost so much faith in ourselves. We have subscribed to models of relationships that are more about giving up our power than cultivating our own power.

In the past,
we ask God to help us to heal
we ask holy people, ancestors, deities
believing they have answers for us.

We act as if everything is outside,
but now we have to reconnect with who we are.
We can talk to our body,
our spirit.

Now, it's about finding out who we are.

I started feeling better, when I had started understanding more of who I am.
At the end of the day, it's about us finding and understanding ourselves.

If we were totally connected to ourselves, we would have so many answers, like what we need to heal.

We need to really trust ourselves
and have a connection to the bigger picture,
which means letting go
of so much of what we have learnt.
Understanding that there is a Creator
and we are part of that Creation,
knowing that we are never alone here
and that beyond what we see and touch,
there is more!

It's ok that we worship our own Gods and we will be tolerant and respectful of those who worship different from us. However, we are all part of the Creation.

We can say "that's your truth, and I accept and respect that" as opposed to insisting that they accept our truth.

I looked across at him. I looked at his eyes. They were moist with tears, but there was also a beautiful golden light with a sepia tone coming from them.

Once again, I saw him reach into his pouch. He pulled out a piece of paper. It was carefully folded. He handed it to me and said:
"This is a gift for you. This is a prayer made by a spiritual teacher I had, Bilal Ware."

He handed me the paper. When it touched my hands, I could feel the paper was well-worn. It had obviously been referred to many many times.

I took it and bowed to him
with the paper clasped in my hand
and then I touched it
to my forehead.

(As I did this, I realized that this was what I saw spiritual people in India do when they received offerings and gifts.)

I carefully unfolded the paper.
It had sepia coloured words and images on it
alongside the image of a West African woman
and the figure of a Black man
with his upper torso and head wrapped in white cloth
with his face only partially revealed.

As I looked at the images, trying to identify them, I heard him say,

"That picture is taken in Senegal. That woman is Senegalese and the man in the white garment is a representation of the Senegalese Saint Cheik Amadou Bamba."

I looked down to read the text
written alongside the images.

The text read:

This is a supplication I have made
"Please put me in the place
where I can make the most benefit
to the most people
so I can undo the harm
I have done to my own soul"
- Dr Butch Bilal Ware

I read it
and I read it again
and I read it again and again

Each time I read the words
"so I can undo the harm
I have done to my own soul"
I felt something moving in my spirit.
I couldn't stop repeating
because when I read,
I felt a sense of completion
A sense of a closing of a cycle.
Now I could truly move forward.

I had received a special spiritual guideline.
Now it was my turn for my eyes to be filled with tears.
I looked up from reading the paper to thank the man.
However, he was no longer in front of me.

I looked all around me.
He was no longer in my sight.

I immediately realised that he had continued on his journey.
I also immediately knew what else I had to do.

I wiped my tears and reached in my small backpack and took
out some tobacco and sage that I had.

I placed them at the spot where he had been sitting
and made a prayer,
giving thanks to all the forces of Creation,
the guardians of the land I was on,

all the ancestral spirits
that had facilitated
my reaching this sacred place
and enabling this dialogue
to take place
which marked the end of one journey and cycle of life
and the start and beginning of a new journey and cycle of life.

I knew I was stepping into a new future
where there would be less people afraid of death
where I could make new agreements
about how I could conduct relationships
where I could take more responsibility
assume more of my own power
where I could heal myself
and break the chain of traumas
passed on through generations.

What made this even more powerful for me
was that I realized I would not be alone.
There would be other fearless ones
charting new pathways
determined by the dictates of their own hearts.

It was a time to move forward.
It was a truly joyous moment!

"Please put me in the place where I can make the most benefit, to the most people, so I can undo the harm I have done to my own soul."

★

Dr Butch Bilal Ware

Ge'ez

Heran ★ Blen ★ Amenti ★ Hannah

yemi

www.ingramcontent.com/pod-product-compliance
Lightning Source LLC
Chambersburg PA
CBHW041928040426
42444CB00018B/3465